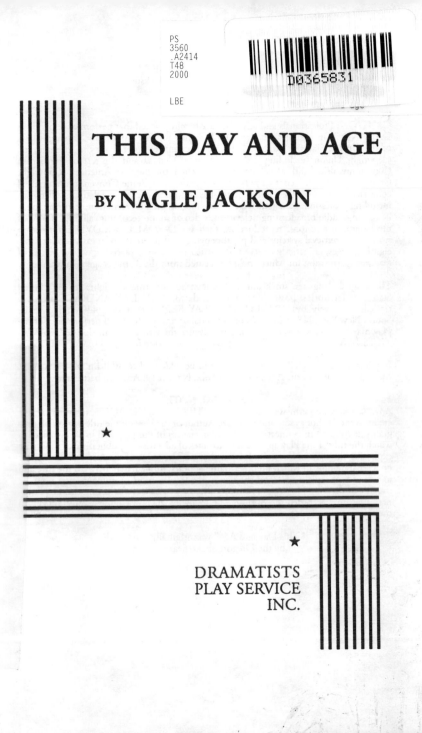

THIS DAY AND AGE

BY NAGLE JACKSON

DRAMATISTS
PLAY SERVICE
INC.

THIS DAY AND AGE
Copyright © 2000, Nagle Jackson

All Rights Reserved

THIS DAY AND AGE was produced by the Oregon Shakespeare Festival (Henry Woronicz, Artistic Director) on April 23, 1995. It was directed by Pat Patton; the set design was by William Bloodgood; the lighting design was by Dawn Chiang; the costume design was by Susan Mickey; and the music director was Todd Barton. The cast was as follows:

MARJORIE	Susan Corzatte
ANN	Robin Goodrin Nordli
BRIAN	James Newcomb
JOY	Bonnie Akimoto
TONY	Raymond L. Chapman
THE MAN	Clayton Corzatte

3

CHARACTERS

MARJORIE, just turned 60 and has no problem with that at all.
ANN, 30-ish. Marjorie's efficient, professional daughter.
BRIAN, Ann's husband, a bit older, British.
TONY, late 20s; Marjorie's son.
JOY, about 30, Asian-American; Tony's wife. Former dancer.
THE MAN, 60s.

PLACE

The patio of Marjorie's upscale suburban home in Connecticut.

TIME

The present.

THIS DAY AND AGE

SCENE ONE

Summer, outdoors. A patio by the swimming pool, which we do not see but only hear from time to time, offstage right. On the patio, summer furniture: a recliner, chairs, a large, round, white metal table with umbrella. Seated at this table, reading: Marjorie, a handsome woman who has just turned sixty and has no problems with that at all. She is dressed smartly, with a lightweight beach robe hanging loosely over all. She puts down a book and speaks to someone off right.

MARJORIE. Talk to me this afternoon, Jack. They'll be gone after lunch I expect. They don't expect, but I expect. They'll be furious, or "wounded," or maybe just concerned for mother's mental stability, but they'll want to leave. To decamp. And regroup. *(Pause.)* You give them too much credit, Jack. They won't "understand," of that I am quite sure. Well, it is hard news, maybe. But I don't see, really don't see why it should be. Not in this day and age. You got out just in time, boy-o. You sly dog. Eleven o'clock. Time for your swim … No, I'm not going in today. I have more than enough stimulation to look forward to as is. *(A car driving into a driveway, offstage L.)* See? Right on time. Annie is nothing if not punctual. I know. She gets it from you.
ANN. *(Offstage.)* Hi!
MARJORIE. Out here! I'm not getting out of this chair. *(Pause.)* Problem?
ANN. *(Offstage.)* No. *(Pause.)* Yes. *(Ann enters. She is her mother's daughter, early thirties, wears sensible, simple clothing that costs a lot.*

5

She carries an enormous purse.) It's that damned fascist car we bought in Düsseldorf. Hi, mom. *(She kisses Marjorie on the cheek.)*

MARJORIE. Hi, dear. Well, it got you here on time.

ANN. Yes, but it talked to us all the way, and Bri's going crazy trying to translate.

MARJORIE. A talking car?

ANN. Oh god, yes. It's the new thing, you know. Instead of just having little lights come on and tell you if you're too hot or out of oil or whatever, now they've got these recorded messages that *tell* you to buckle up, release the brake, turn your lights out. But, see, we bought this one over there, so it speaks German, and it always sounds like you're being arrested.

BRIAN. *(Offstage.)* Do you have a German dictionary in the house?

MARJORIE. Yes! I think so. Look in the den.

BRIAN. *(Offstage.)* Thanks.

MARJORIE. Shelf above the typewriter!

BRIAN. *(Offstage.)* Righty-o!

MARJORIE. *(To Ann.)* Can't you get it fixed?

ANN. Lube, oil change, and a literal translation? I don't think so.

MARJORIE. I wouldn't like a car talking to me, anyway. No matter what its persuasion.

ANN. I don't know. A chatty Peugeot might be fun, how are you?

MARJORIE. Mmm. Nice.

ANN. Were you surprised when we asked to come?

MARJORIE. No. But I was surprised when Tony and Joy asked to come on the same day.

ANN. You're kidding.

MARJORIE. Any moment now.

ANN. They didn't tell me that. Did you tell them we were coming?

MARJORIE. Tony said, "Fine."

ANN. Tony always says "fine." "Fine" is the great shield of the McDermotts. Up to your ears in quicksand? "Fine."

MARJORIE. It comes from a desire not to burden other people with one's little problems.

ANN. It *comes* from a desire to appear perfect.

MARJORIE. You said you had something to tell me ...

ANN. Are they bringing the kids?

6

MARJORIE. No, something to tell me; do you want to wait till the others are here?

ANN. Damn.

MARJORIE. What's wrong?

ANN. Well, I don't know if I want to wait or not, now that they're coming. I had hoped we could have a drink — well, not me, I don't drink anymore — but, I mean just sort of cool down and maybe have some lunch. Well, not me, I don't do lunch anymore.

MARJORIE. Sort of news that needs to be cushioned?

ANN. No, not really.

MARJORIE. Well, I'm going to have an eye-opener anyhow.

ANN. An "eye-opener"? At eleven in the morning?

MARJORIE. Jack always called them eye-openers until it was time to say "the sun had passed over the yard-arm" — whatever a yard-arm is …

ANN. *(Going to the drink table.)* Do you have all the stuff out here? The drink stuff?

MARJORIE. We'll need ice.

ANN. I'll get it.

MARJORIE. It's your party.

ANN. What's that supposed to mean?

MARJORIE. I mean you "called the meeting."

ANN. Is it a bad time?

MARJORIE. It's a perfect time. Really.

ANN. I hope so. *(Brian enters — from L. He is somewhat older than Ann and looks even more so because of his elegant gray hair. His clothes look very British because both they, and he, are.)*

BRIAN. The *kofferaum*, thank you very much, is the boot. I mean the trunk. The bloody trunk wasn't latched. That's what the *führer* in the dashboard was telling us. Hello, Marjorie. *(He kisses her.)*

MARJORIE. Hello, Brian. How are you?

BRIAN. Well, now that I know we're not being deported to Poland, I'm fine.

ANN *(Leaving.)* I'll get ice. Tony and Joy are coming over.

BRIAN *(Pleased.)* Really! *(Ann exits, L. To Marjorie.)* You look sublime.

MARJORIE. I feel sublime. I really do.

BRIAN. Has Ann talked to you?

MARJORIE. No. She says we have to grease the gears first. Toddies, lunch ...

BRIAN. Isn't she odd? This woman storms the Environmental Protection Agency on an almost daily basis, badgers polluters for sport, and is terrified to talk to her own mother.

MARJORIE. She just had another scenario in mind. You know Annie: everything mapped out.

BRIAN. Yes, well ... How's the pool?

MARJORIE Fine.

BRIAN. Looks good.

MARJORIE. Actually, I've had a spot of trouble ... I love it when you come over, Brian. I start to say things like "spot of trouble" ... but anyway, there's a pool man who's supposed to come and take its temperature and give it a dose of salts or whatever. Mr. Palestrina. Isn't that elegant? Palestrina ... But he missed last week ... *(Pause.)* ... or I didn't see him if he came. *(Ann enters from the house, L. with an ice bucket.)*

ANN. Your fridge is a mess. You've got stuff in there from last Christmas.

MARJORIE. I do not.

ANN. Those green tomato pickles that Joy gave you?

MARJORIE. Oh, those.

ANN. And there's a brand of ice cream I don't think they even make anymore.

MARJORIE. You stay out of my fridge. Bri, make us drinks.

ANN. I'll make them. Brian makes drinks like they do in England. Teeny bits of gin and warm tonic.

BRIAN. We invented it, my dear. And if you want a large, you order a large. And you don't drink anyway, so I'll make the drinks. *(To Marjorie.)* G and T's I presume, Madame?

MARJORIE. Absolutely. *(Ann reaches into her enormous bag and pulls out a large bottle of mineral water.)*

ANN. Here. For me.

MARJORIE. What on earth is that?

ANN. It's new ... I love it ... It's from a spring in Ithaca.

MARJORIE. Ithaca! *(Marjorie sings.)* "High above Cayuga's Waters, comes an awful smell" ... I thought.

BRIAN. *(Handing drink to Marjorie.)* Here you are. And Annie can have her minerals, and then she can tell you her news. Our news.

MARJORIE. Dear god, you're not pregnant? *(Ann stops dead in her tracks. She drops the bottle of mineral water.)*

ANN. I cannot *believe* you said that.

MARJORIE. *(Wearily.)* Oh dear ...

BRIAN. *(Looking at drained bottle.)* So much for Ithaca.

ANN. In fact, Brian and I have decided to adopt.

MARJORIE. And does the Green Conservancy have someone to replace you?

ANN. I don't need to be replaced.

MARJORIE. I see. You are adopting an eighteen-year-old perhaps.

ANN. Oh, for Christ's sake!

MARJORIE. Because unless you are, you will find that the endless round of day-care centers, babysitters, et cetera, et cetera, while you pretend to be a parent, can be pretty wearing.

ANN. I am not pretending to be a parent.

MARJORIE. Then you, Brian; are you leaving the station?

BRIAN. Of course not. I may switch to a different shift. We're shuffling the whole program schedule around soon. Well ... in February.

MARJORIE. I think you're both being wildly unrealistic.

ANN. Is *that* all? I thought you were going to say the world doesn't need any more children —

MARJORIE. It doesn't.

ANN. But that doesn't apply because we're taking one who's already in it.

MARJORIE. I just think that, in this day and age, it is not absolutely necessary for everyone to be a parent. I thought we were getting away from all that. And, Ann, you live in *Manhattan*. You've got a life; not a function. My god, I always wanted to live in Manhattan. I remember Madge Sylvester and I were getting on yet another train home after yet another matinee ... that nice play with Margaret Leighton. Well, anyway, I said: "Wouldn't it be very heaven to go to an evening performance and just take a cab home?" She disagreed, of course, because she likes golf, but you don't like golf, Ann; you've got a mind.

9

ANN. And I also want to have a family.

MARJORIE. "Family"! The "F" word. Why do people go on and on about "family values"? Most of the families I know are bastions of self-interest and breeding grounds for neuroses. What values are those?

ANN. Mother ...

MARJORIE. And I hate family restaurants because they always have bottles of ketchup everywhere and no bar.

ANN. *Mother* ...

MARJORIE. Eighty percent of the population should never be allowed to rear children in the first place. Of course, the more ill-equipped they are for the job, the more likely they are to take it on. Nature's vast practical joke. Or evolution's sly way of wearing out the race.

ANN. I hope I never arrive at such a bitter view of the world.

MARJORIE. Not bitter. Objective. And it comes with age.

ANN. God save us from angry old people. And they vote!

MARJORIE. Only ones who do. But I resent your terminology.

BRIAN. Yes. Marjorie will never be old.

MARJORIE. Oh, I am old. Thank goodness. No, it's the "angry" part I object to. If you think I sit here like Queen Lear railing against my fry, or the young in general, you are very much mistaken. I have many better ways to die. *(Pause.)* Look, you're an ecology advocate. You've tried for years to get pregnant and nothing's happened. Might that not be part of Nature's plan? Maybe there's some reason you're not supposed to be a mother.

ANN. Thank you very much!

MARJORIE. It's a highly over-rated profession, believe me. Now, Brian, you have tried everything?

BRIAN. All the gynecological tricks. Some of which were rather fun, actually. And some of which were not.

MARJORIE. So you're going to adopt something, fine. And then you're going to line up a battery of nannies and housekeepers, etcetera, etcetera. I hope you have enough money for all this.

ANN. Well, you see ... that's another reason we want to get out of Manhattan.

BRIAN. Life would be ... cheaper ... in the suburbs.

MARJORIE. In every way, yes. Will you go south to New Jersey

10

or north to Connecticut? *(Pause.)*

BRIAN. Well ... we're still in the planning stages of course, but ...

ANN. We thought we'd move here.

MARJORIE. Oh, Ann, you'll never be able to afford a thing around here. Will Perry and I were talking the other day — you remember Will. Real estate for ages. He tells me prices here are obscene.

ANN. No, we mean *here*. *(Pause. The penny drops.)*

MARJORIE. Here?! For heaven's sake, why would you want to ... No.

ANN. *(Disbelief.)* No?!

MARJORIE. Absolutely no.

ANN. We thought you'd be thrilled. You've been out here all by your lonesome since Dad died.

MARJORIE. What's that got to do with anything?

ANN. Whoever heard of anyone wanting to be all alone?

MARJORIE. Anyone who's tried it. Why would you think I wish to be surrounded by kith and kin? *(The sound of a car driving in.)* Ah, here come some more kith.

ANN. That's Tony and Joy. I can't see them now. *(She starts to leave.)*

BRIAN. Ann ...

ANN. *(Coming back.)* And not a word of all this to them!

MARJORIE. Why ever not?

ANN. Because it's all just ... just too awful! *(She runs out, probably in tears.)*

TONY. *(Offstage.)* "Hi, Annie!" *(Silence.)*

MARJORIE. Brian, this couldn't have been your idea.

BRIAN. Oh no, you're not getting me into that discussion. *(Joy enters. L. She is about thirty and is Asian-American. She has lots of jet black hair tied in a knot and cascading down her back.)*

JOY. What's the matter with Ann? Hi, Marjorie.

MARJORIE. Hello, darling. *(Joy comes over and kisses her on the cheek.)* Don't worry about Ann; she's a big girl.

JOY. Hi, Brian.

BRIAN. *(He goes to Joy and kisses her.)* Hello, you gorgeous thing. Ann's not very pleased with things, because they didn't go as planned. In her head. You know.

JOY. Oh. *(Pause.)* You've told me nothing. Anyway, Tony's gone in to see her. I know I should too, probably. But I'm no good at that. *(She sits.)*

MARJORIE. There's no need to make a fuss. No need for anyone to go to her. There's far too much of that sort of thing nowadays.

BRIAN. What sort of thing?

MARJORIE. "Going to help," sort of thing. People thrive on it. Everyone wants to get in on the grief. It's called "caring;" really just ego-feeding.

BRIAN. You want a drink, Joy?

JOY. Sure. You know, one of Petie's classmates was killed in an auto accident. And it was awful, of course, but Petie was fine. He was fascinated, but he was fine. Then, the school brought in professional counselors for the kids. To help them "deal with their grief." I don't know.

MARJORIE. Vultures. Ready to feed on the general malaise. No inner resources left, you see. Run to counselors for marital unrest, social unrest, economic unrest; who on earth said people were supposed to be at rest?

JOY. Still, I've never known Annie to … She looked like she was crying.

BRIAN. Oh, Annie cries. I am happy to report that Annie is subject to most of the thousand natural shocks that flesh is heir to. *(To Marjorie.)* You knocked the wind out of her, old girl.

MARJORIE. Please don't call me "old girl." Only one man was ever allowed to call me that, and he's dead.

BRIAN. Sorry.

MARJORIE. So, Petie has been counseled and survived. And how is our little princess?

JOY. Pam is great. But I really don't know many princesses who pick their nose. *(Tony enters. He is wearing a sport jacket that doesn't seem necessary. He is Ann's younger brother, trim, fit, but fiddles with things a lot — his glasses, his right sideburn, which is curly and which he tugs at and twirls. He probably used to smoke. His attention span is rather limited.)*

TONY. She'll be right out. Hi, Mother. *(Kisses Marjorie hello.)*

MARJORIE Hello, dear.

TONY. Hello, Brian. We were really pleased to hear you and

Annie'd be here, too. Boy, I've never seen her that upset. She just stormed right past me.

BRIAN. Ann's under a wee bit of stress at the moment. She'll tell you all about it. What say to a drink?

TONY. Oh no. No thanks. Don't do that anymore.

MARJORIE. Not you too? What's a mother to do? And dear Lolly, who's been my bar-mate at the Country Club for a hundred and fifty years, has joined AA.

TONY. Good for her. Nothing to be ashamed of.

MARJORIE. Ashamed? All our old friends seem positively to revel in it. "It's just a disease, Marjorie." Well, yes, that's as may be, but isn't it rather odd that every person within a five-mile radius has come down with it? I swear I shall end up sipping sherry by my lonesome and being no fun at all.

TONY. Oh, we won't let that happen.

BRIAN. You'll always have me, Mother Brown.

MARJORIE. *(Lifting her empty glass.)* Knees up.

BRIAN. I'll fix you. *(He goes to drink table.)*

TONY. Is there anything besides tonic? Wait a minute ... *(A revelation.)* I think I'll have tonic.

MARJORIE. There was something ghastly from Ithaca, but it went away.

TONY. Oh. *(Pause. Tony pours himself a tonic. Brian fixes Marjorie's drink and his own.)*

JOY. I might go for a swim.

MARJORIE. Oh good! It needs to be kicked up. I haven't been in for days.

TONY. *(Looking off R.)* Mother.

MARJORIE. What?

TONY. It looks *green.*

MARJORIE. It does not. Now, Tony, you are always finding something wrong with my lovely pool.

TONY. I love your lovely pool, but I think it's turning —

MARJORIE. You have always had a problem with the colors blue and green.

TONY. Mother, I was an *Art* major.

MARJORIE. I don't care about that. You used to call your green sweaters blue and your blue socks green. I remember vividly your

13

going out one St. Patrick's Day looking like Gainsborough's Blue Boy. Several Catholics beat you up.

TONY. Mother, I think the pool needs some chemicals or something.

MARJORIE. You just think I can't take care of my pool.

TONY. I thought you had a man to do that.

MARJORIE. I do. Mister Palestrina. *(Brian laughs.)*

TONY. And he's ripping you off. It's not your fault. You shouldn't have to run this whole damn place yourself. It was easy when Dad was alive; he loved taking care of the pool.

JOY. *(Smiling.)* I know. He'd never let anyone *swim* in it. He was always testing it or vacuuming it. Mmm, I miss him. I really do.

BRIAN. *(Lifting his glass.)* Here's to Jack.

MARJORIE. It did give him a great deal of pleasure. And I swear it lengthened his life by at least five years. You know we were supposed to lose him after the second attack, but no. He swam his laps every day. I'm sure it helped.

TONY. Anyway, you shouldn't have to worry about all these things.

MARJORIE. I agree. I couldn't agree more. *(Pause.)*

JOY. I'm going to put on my suit. *(Ann suddenly appears from L.)*

ANN. If you *must* know, Brian and I have decided to adopt. *(Pause.)*

A child.

JOY. *(Going to her.)* Ah, Annie, that's great!

ANN. My name is Ann.

JOY. Oh …

ANN. When I'm upset.

TONY. Why are you upset? I think it's fine. Isn't that fine, mother?

ANN. Mother thinks it's dumb. Hi, Joy. I'm sorry to snap at you.

JOY. Oh, that's okay. You're probably just feeling "pregnant" … I'm going swimming. *(She exits, L.)*

MARJORIE. I don't think it's "dumb" — whatever that may mean. I just think it's unnecessary.

ANN. Was it "necessary" for you to be a mother?

MARJORIE. Yes, it was. There were no options in those days. The men were out hunting and gathering, and we stayed home to tend the fire. It never occurred to anyone to leave the cave except to play bridge. I know it sounds disgusting ... because it was.

TONY. Are you saying? ... You mean you didn't want us?

MARJORIE. Oh, I cried and cried, and everyone said "Isn't it touching, she's so happy she's actually weeping with joy." And I bought right into it. No, Tony, it isn't that I didn't *want* you ... I mean once you were there. I've just never been given those maternal hormones, I guess.

TONY. You were a wonderful mother!

MARJORIE. Of course I was. I do everything well. Doesn't mean I enjoy it. And, Ann, I don't think you really want to be a mother. You just think it's chic. Like marrying a Brit.

ANN. Chic?!

MARJORIE. You read far too many magazines, Ann. I've often said so.

ANN. You're just jealous because I've got options. The fact is, I *can* have it all!

MARJORIE. And you've always wanted it all, haven't you?

ANN. Dad taught me that.

TONY. I'll say ...

BRIAN. Look, "the times they are a changin'," I think we all know that. Ann would like to have a child; I would like to have a child. And of course we both want our careers as well. Not that that's a choice anymore. In these difficult times ...

MARJORIE. These are not difficult times. Really, Brian, that cliché is beneath you. Every politician in the world begins his remarks with a reference to "these difficult times." Now, the Black Plague and the Hundred Years' War, *those* were difficult times.

TONY. I bet the pH balance is off.

ANN. What?!

TONY. The pool. I think it's turning green.

MARJORIE. Tony ... ah, dear Tony. Listen, you said you had some news for me as well. What is it?

TONY. Oh ... well, it's rather complicated.

MARJORIE. *(To Brian and Ann.)* You see, right after Ann phoned, Tony phoned and said he had something he wanted to tell me as well. It is to be a day of great moments. *(Joy enters, looking smashing in a bathing suit.)* Now, Joy. You're not pregnant are you?

15

JOY. *(Crossing to R.)* Heaven forbid. *(She exits.)*

MARJORIE. Good.

BRIAN. Tony, you're pregnant.

TONY. Ha, ha. No. It's a bit more complicated than that.

BRIAN. I can't think of anything more complicated than that.

TONY. It's just … well, I look at this big, old place, and I see things … well, things that need to be … and Mom is just sitting here all alone, and … Oh, hell, I'll just come right out with it: *(He takes Marjorie's hand.)* Mom, we've decided to come out here and move in with you. *(Pause. Offstage: a loud splash. Joy has dived in.)*

BRIAN. Women amaze me. They way they can just do that. Dive in, like that.

ANN. Shut up, Brian.

MARJORIE. My, aren't we having a good old time at grand-mother's house today.

TONY. Is anything the matter? *(Ann sits. To Marjorie.)* I thought you'd be thrilled.

MARJORIE. Have you heard? Have you *listened* to one word I have been saying?

TONY. Sure. You mean about Ann adopting kids and stuff?

MARJORIE. Well, mainly the "stuff." My maternal hormones. Stuff like that.

TONY. Oh. *(Pause.)* But you love our kids.

MARJORIE. Of course I love your kids. Everyone loves kids who go home.

ANN. You have got some nerve, Tony. I know this wasn't Joy's idea.

MARJORIE. *(Looking off R.)* Look at the way she swims laps. It's that oriental work ethic.

TONY. Mother, Joy is not "oriental." She was born in the sovereign state of Hawaii. She was a cheerleader, for god's sake. She's as American as —

BRIAN. Pineapple pie.

ANN. I do not believe Joy wants to leave your perfectly nice house in New Rochelle —

TONY. Well … it's not all that easy.

ANN. What's not all that easy?

TONY. Life in New Rochelle. Life in New Rochelle is not that easy.

MARJORIE. Who said life was supposed to be easy?

ANN. Have you lost another job?

TONY. No!

BRIAN. Ann, is this really the time or the place?

ANN. It is precisely the time. It is precisely the place. He wants to just move in here, and …

MARJORIE *(To her.)* Well, so do you.

TONY. What?! … Aha! So that's the game. Super-Ann has a super-plan!

MARJORIE. *(To Brian.)* This is what "sibling" means.

TONY. You've got a wonderful career going … environmental lawyer, all the rage … Brian's with the best classical music station in New York … What on earth do you *want?*

ANN. And you've got two adorable children, a beautiful, intelligent wife who actually enjoys being wife and mommy; you've got a nice enough little house in the suburbs, what on earth do you want? You have lost your job, haven't you?

TONY. I have not lost my job. But it's … well, it no longer challenges me.

MARJORIE. And now that cliché.

ANN. So you want to live out here and sponge off mom. That's the bottom line here.

TONY. I would never do that!

ANN. Sounds like it to me. Look, you're too young to have a mid-life crisis, so you must be broke.

TONY. What I want to know is why you and Brian want to come here and "sponge off Mom" as you put it.

ANN. We have no intention of sponging off Mom. We would more than pay our way. And we would run the place for her, so she could just relax.

TONY. Oh, I see it all now. You're going to get in here, grab the property and hold on for dear life, aren't you? And you're pretending it's out of filial concern. My god, what … what chicanery!

BRIAN. Even I resent that. And I almost never resent anything.

TONY. So, we're right back to Mr. Sandusky's swing!

ANN. Oh, please!

BRIAN. Who?

TONY. It is. It is exactly Mr. Sandusky's swing all over again.

MARJORIE. *(To Brian.)* Mr. Sandusky lived on the next property. He was very sweet and rather strange.

TONY. I discovered that swing, you know.

ANN. You discovered a tire hanging on a rope from a tree. I discovered the potential.

TONY. It was a perfectly good swing before you turned it into some kind of *challenge*.

ANN. It was much more fun swinging out over the creek.

TONY. Yes, that was okay, but who thought up the bit about jumping out of the swing and into the water below. Who had to "Tarzan" it up like that?

ANN. It was fun.

TONY. And then you made it a rule: No one could use the Sanduskys' swing unless they swung out over the creek and jumped in. And I didn't want to do that. So, just because I don't enjoy swimming —

ANN. You can't swim.

TONY. Can too!

ANN. No you can't. You just wave your hands around like a puppy dog and go "wuppa, wuppa, wuppa"! *(She demonstrates dog-paddle.)*

TONY. *(To Brian.)* She established a reign of terror on Mr. Sandusky's swing.

ANN. And you fell for it!

TONY. Joy! Stop swimming in that pool, it's unclean! *(Pause.)* Ann does this all the time; someone gets an idea and then she just takes it over.

MARJORIE. That is what capitalism means. Don't be unpatriotic, dear.

ANN. You are an incompetent, Tony. And I am a competent. It all boils down to that.

TONY. Well, I can't be totally incompetent; at least I'm able to make babies.

ANN. You son of a bitch! *(She throws a beach towel at him.)*

MARJORIE. Now there's an interesting role-reversal. It always was Tony who used to throw things at people. For instance, he threw that electric pencil sharpener —

TONY. Mother! ... Look, why don't you do that foster parent

thing? We've done that. You know, we send money in every month and we've got this little girl in Ecuador named Maria-something-something. They've all got two last names in Ecuador. You'd fit right in.

ANN. What's that supposed to mean?

TONY. Well, you go around with your hyphenated last names, don't you?

ANN. *Our* hyphenated last name. I certainly do.

MARJORIE. I have found that after five years or so, most women either drop the hyphen or drop the marriage. Why shilly-shally with things? *(Pause.)*

BRIAN. "Shilly-shally" is hyphenated, I believe.

ANN. We are not joining a foster parent plan. We are not sending a monthly check to Ecuador or Bangladesh — though I think that's admirable, I really do. We are adopting a child.

TONY. Fine. I think that's fine. Insofar as it goes. So does Joy. She thinks it's fine. I don't know why mother has a problem with that.

MARJORIE. Mother is not going to have a problem with that. But Ann will, and she ought to think it through.

ANN. Like, we just now came up with this and haven't given it a great deal of thought already! *(Pause.)*

MARJORIE. Yes?

ANN. Yes, what?

MARJORIE. I am waiting for the rest of your sentence. Phrases beginning with "Like" — as in "Like we just now thought of this" — are subordinate clauses merely, "like" being a clumsy substitute for "as if." I am waiting for the main clause.

ANN. *(Livid with anger.)* Well, you can wait till hell freezes over! And the bloody pool turns *blue! (Ann starts to exit — Joy enters wet from her swim.)*

JOY. Can everyone just relax? Why don't you all go for a swim?

BRIAN. Ah, the voice of reason. Hawaiian reason.

TONY. I'm sure the pH balance is off. I'm going to check. You really shouldn't be swimming in that muck.

JOY. That muck is divine. *(Tony exits to the pool.)* Ann, you'll make a wonderful mother. I think it's great. *(She goes to Ann and embraces her.)* ... And I'm sorry I'm wet.

ANN. Joy, you're a sensible person. You can't really want to move out here with mother, can you?

MARJORIE. I move we table that discussion. Why don't you do as Joy says and swim? Or get some sun?

ANN. I don't do that anymore. Skin cancer

MARJORIE. What a lovely thought, we're *so* pleased. Well, lunch will be arriving soon. I telephoned Cuisine Courante because they do such nice things, and I've learned to hate the kitchen since Jack died. Isn't that awful?

JOY. No. I look forward to hating the kitchen.

TONY. *(From off R.)* Thank you very much! *(Brian has settled himself in a deck chair and is drifting off into a nap. Joy sits.)*

ANN. I've got stuff to do.

MARJORIE. Oh dear, work?

BRIAN. *(Eyes closed.)* Trees ...

MARJORIE. Well, before you get involved in that ... And, well, so perhaps you'll understand some of my concerns ...

ANN. Mother, just drop it.

MARJORIE. No, no. Nothing to do with you, dear. Well, yes, quite a lot to do with you actually. With all of you. I've got some news, too.

BRIAN. *(Waking up.)* Don't tell us *you're* pregnant?

MARJORIE. Yes, and a very old star shone in the East. No, it's just that ... it's just that I have come to a decision. I mentioned hating the kitchen. And the truth is I really don't even enjoy the pool that much anymore.

JOY. *(Nervous.)* Marjorie ...

MARJORIE. Well, it's not all that unusual for us widow-ladies to pull up stakes, is it?

ANN. *(Sitting up.)* Oh, no. You're not going to move into some dreary condo?!

MARJORIE. No, no. I won't be ordinary, Ann, if I can help it. But I have decided to move.

BRIAN. Really!

MARJORIE. Yes — *(In an off-handed manner.)* — to New Zealand. *(Offstage R. the sound of a splash.)*

JOY. *(Matter-of-factly.)* Tony fell into the pool ...

BRIAN. Have you ever ...

ANN. Mother —

BRIAN. Have you ever been to New Zealand?

ANN. Mother, that is the silliest ... Don and Marge Williams moved to New Zealand, and they said it was like living in the '50s.

MARJORIE. I enjoyed the fifties. Except for McCarthy. And Arthur Godfrey. I met Jack in the fifties. In Philadelphia, at the Mask and Wig.

BRIAN. Whereabouts in New Zealand, Marjorie?

MARJORIE. I shall fly to Auckland and stay in a residential hotel for a while, getting the feel of the place ...

BRIAN. That will take about fifteen minutes.

MARJORIE. Don't be rude about New Zealand, Brian.

BRIAN. I've been there. It's very beautiful. It's very peaceful. You are far too interesting for Auckland, Marjorie.

MARJORIE. I intend to see Wellington, too. But I've made reservations for Auckland. *(Tony enters, dripping wet.)*

TONY. You've got reservations?! *(Joy starts to giggle, and her laughter will increase steadily.)*

MARJORIE. I have. Tony, you're all wet.

TONY. Oh my god! Tickets and everything?

MARJORIE. Tickets and everything.

TONY. But what about *this* place?

MARJORIE. I've spoken with Will Perry at the real estate agency. He says it will "sell in a minute."

ANN. Sell?!

MARJORIE. Even in "these difficult times."

TONY. The estate? Sell?! Sell the estate??

MARJORIE. What *are* you laughing at, Joy?

TONY. She's laughing at me.

JOY. I'm sorry.

TONY. Certain things set her off and she can't stop: People falling down ... wet people. *(Joy whoops with laughter.)* Old people falling down really slay her. Last week we saw —

ANN. *(To Marjorie.)* I cannot believe you would go and sell the family estate without consulting us.

MARJORIE. Well, you've got homes. You've got lives. I knew you'd just kick up a fuss — as you are doing —

TONY. But our homes are ... They're small.

MARJORIE. That is life, my dear. The gradual decline, or —

well, change. You see the sad thing is, the American Dream happened. Which none of us really wanted. Ann doesn't want it, because people need to chop down trees to build it. Tony doesn't want it because it means more neighbors and smaller houses. I sit here, presiding over the Decline and Fall, and I'd really rather not. I'd rather do that at a distance.

ANN. Wait a minute, wait a minute. I'm not going to take this seriously. This is some whim of yours ...

TONY. *(To Brian.)* I knew this sort of thing would happen with her living all alone.

ANN. Well, exactly. Now lets talk this thing out and ... I mean, I think a good, long vacation in New Zealand would be wonderful for you.

TONY. Absolutely. *(Joy has stopped laughing.)*

MARJORIE. Vacation from what? No, Annie, you won't bully me out of anything this time.

TONY. But look, Mom ... even if you did decide to live in New Zealand ... or London ... or Timbuktu ... there's no reason to sell the house!

MARJORIE. There is every reason. I want the money.

TONY. *(Weakly.)* What?

MARJORIE. I want the money. To buy something nice in New Zealand and live rather well.

ANN. You've got money.

MARJORIE. Oh yes. Jack took care of me. The royalties still come in. But things are dreadfully expensive nowadays.

BRIAN. In these difficult times.

TONY. But ... You mean you're just going to ... spend it? Dip into ... capital?

MARJORIE. Yes. *(Pause.)* I want to. *(Pause.)* Oh, don't worry. There'll be a little something left over for you. But don't count on that. Don't rely on it. Don't be selfish.

TONY. Selfish?!

ANN. Selfish?!

ANN and TONY. *(Together.)* Us!!

JOY. Tony, you have got to change.

TONY. Huh?

JOY. Your clothes. Did your wallet get soaked?

22

TONY. Doesn't matter. Everything's plastic. *(Pause.)*
BRIAN. New Bloody Zealand. Christ.
MARJORIE. So, that's my news.
ANN. And our adopted child will have to go to New Zealand to see his grandmother.
BRIAN. His?
ANN. Or hers. Whatever.
BRIAN. I do hope "hers."
JOY. Really Brian, why?
BRIAN. Oh god, boys! You have to play baseball and go fishing and all that sort of gee-whiz stuff. Little girls just love their daddies and you buy them things.
JOY. That is the most sexist thing I have ever heard.
MARJORIE. And it's not true, either. Annie was the athlete in this family. And Tony, come to think of it, did like us to buy him things.
TONY. What are we talking about? Children? Mother is throwing away our — our life ... our past, our entire childhood —
MARJORIE. The past goes away, Tony. And your childhood, I'm sorry to point out, is over.
TONY. But our kids. Pam and Petie...
MARJORIE. You're giving them a childhood. Aren't you?
JOY. You know, Petie wasn't really all that upset when I said they couldn't come with us today.
TONY. He's just pretending. He does that to annoy me. *(He sits in despair.)* Oh my *god.*
MARJORIE. Joy, is Ann right? Has Tony lost his job?
TONY. Why are you asking her? No! It's just ... well, I'm really ... less than thrilled with designing books, if you must know.
MARJORIE. We cannot always be thrilled. Jack was less than thrilled with the insurance business. But he kept at it. Even after his songs began to sell. He kept at it. And look at poor Joy; she gave up her dancing career to take care of *you.*
TONY. To take care of the children.
MARJORIE. Same thing, really.
TONY. Okay fine! *(He rises in anger.)* Sell the place. Sell the house and the creek and the swimming pool and the rose garden. Sell the library and the bedrooms and the study and the ... Just sell the

whole damn thing to some nouveau-riche boobs who will ...

MARJORIE. *(Getting annoyed now.)* May I remind you that we are distinctly "nouveau riche"? Well, not quite as "riche" as I'd like, but certainly "nouveau." Your father didn't have a dime back in Pottstown, PA, and went to Penn on scholarship. If you've forgotten that, you've missed the main point. This ... place ... is what one can do with one's life. MAYBE!

ANN. Honestly, Tony!

TONY. All right, all right. Sorry

MARJORIE. The point is ... *(She stands. It is the first time she has risen from her chair.)* The point *is:* Life goes on. And if one is lucky, it goes on and on. And it is discouraging as all hell to have one's children tell you that it shouldn't or it can't. If I just die I'm sure you'd be most pleased. It's my decision to live — and on my terms — that's got you in such a state. Well, I'm sorry, but my mind is made up. *(Offstage L. the sound of a car driving in.)* And I see lunch arriving and I have suddenly developed the appetite of a twelve-year-old! So there! *(Pause.)* Look: Mother stood up. *(Blackout.)*

SCENE TWO

The same. Brian seated on patio. Tony just off right.

BRIAN. Will you stop that? Just leave the pool alone.

TONY. *(Offstage.)* No, I will not. I'm trying to get it stabilized. Get it back to normal.

BRIAN. The symbolism is stupefying.

TONY. *(Entering.)* What symbolism?

BRIAN. Never mind.

TONY. You can be so fucking patronizing with those English vowels.

BRIAN. It's what they pay me for.

TONY. Yes, I suppose it is.

BRIAN. They needed a British accent to compete with that very strange lady on the other classical FM station. She has a sort of indistinguishable, all-purpose European accent. She says things like "concerrrrto," and she can't pronounce the name of Johann Sebastian Bachchchchhhh without vomiting. But New Yorkers love her, so my station hired me to be even more un-American than she.

TONY. How can you stand those hours?

BRIAN. Oh, I'm not there. It's all on tape. I'm home fast asleep with Annie while my voice drones on, supercilious and affected. They couldn't be more pleased.

TONY. I suppose this whole thing doesn't faze you in the least.

BRIAN. Certainly it fazes me. It's a new phase.

TONY. That's all?

BRIAN. Life goes on. Look, I was counting on a bit of this estate too, but economics is economics and I really do think the days of becoming "landed gentry" are over. My friend Bobby Telford over in the UK is heir to a fucking earldom, but the truth of the matter is, his poor daft mum creeps about the upper reaches of the family castle while tourists wander through old pewter downstairs and the whole place will have to be turned over to the realm which, frankly, doesn't even want it anymore because no one can afford it. I mean, if anyone thinks nowadays their lot will be bettered when mum and daddums die … they're living in the past.

TONY. I don't care about the money.

BRIAN. You bloody well do. You want to live off her.

TONY. That is not true!

BRIAN. Well, Joy said you wanted to move in here —

TONY. — and pay our share.

BRIAN. You couldn't afford to. Do you have any idea what the upkeep and taxes are on a place like this?

TONY. There must be some solution.

BRIAN. Why? Because you want it?

TONY. It's just not … Dad would be furious.

BRIAN. How do you know?

TONY. He loved this place.

BRIAN. Of course. And he loved your mother and he loved you and Annie, and he's dead.

TONY. I don't know why I'm even talking to you about this.

BRIAN. *(Grinning.)* 'Cause I'm "family." *(Pause … looking towards the pool.)* That stuff smells foul.

TONY. It does the job. Burning away all the little algae. *(Pause.)* Of course, Mother lives way beyond her means. That's half of it.

BRIAN. Half of what?

TONY. Why she has to move. Why she needs the money and there's … not going to be much left. I mean look at that lunch: catered, for Christ's sake. She could have gone into the kitchen … or Joy could have. But no. It's got to be Cuisine Courante. Some bored housewife running an unnecessary business carting bean soup and alfalfa sprouts all over Connecticut. Jesus.

BRIAN. Yes, why must a slice of ham — excuse me, a slice of *Virginia* ham, which has probably never been anywhere near the Mason-Dixon Line … Why must it be tortured into a croissant? What's wrong with rye? Anyway, it annoys me that croissants are available, nay forced upon one, everywhere. You used to have to go to France. Now they have them at ballparks. They probably have them in New Zealand! *(Pause.)* Well, maybe not.

TONY. She's not really going there.

BRIAN. Oh?

TONY. No. She'll go to Arizona, or maybe up to Maine. She loves Maine.

BRIAN. You don't believe her?

TONY. Mom's been saying a lot of weird things lately. *(Pause.)* I don't mean to suggest she's incompetent …

BRIAN. That's exactly what you mean to suggest, or you wouldn't have said it. Well, you can forget that strategy. Marjorie is sharp as a tack. No, no. That won't do, Tony.

TONY. I didn't mean … I would never dream of … You're sick!

BRIAN. That's as may be, but Marjorie is fine and dandy. *(Joy enters, in bathing suit.)*

JOY. Hi.

BRIAN. Hello, you beautiful thing.

TONY. Is anyone speaking to anyone in there?

JOY. Sure. Lunch made all the difference. I'm a great believer in lunch. *(She exits, R.; we hear a splash.)*

BRIAN. Christ.

TONY. JOY!

BRIAN. She just dives in

TONY. *(Exiting, R.)* Joy, get out of there! It's filled with chemicals!!

JOY. *(Off R.)* It smells awful!

TONY. *(Off R.)* Get out! Get out!

BRIAN. Is she all right?

TONY. *(Entering with Joy.)* I told you I was giving it a shock treatment.

JOY. You couldn't wait till the end of the day!!

TONY. Are you okay?

JOY. I smell like a gas station.

TONY. Take a shower. Right away.

JOY. I really wanted to swim. You just ruined the whole thing.

TONY. I have a responsibility to the pool.

JOY. Not anymore. The pool's going bye-bye.

TONY. You'd love that, wouldn't you!

JOY. I'm going to wash off all *your* pollutants! *(She exits angrily, L.)*

TONY. Great. Now *she's* pissed off at me.

BRIAN. *(Stretching out on recliner.)* She loves you, Tony. They all love you.

TONY. Yes, well … I wish they liked me.

BRIAN. You mustn't expect *too* much. *(Pause.)*

TONY. I called Palestrina.

BRIAN. What?

TONY. The pool man. Left a message on his machine. Now he's going to have to deal with me. *(Pause.)* What'd you guys do on the Fourth of July?

BRIAN. You know, you are quite the oddest bloke I know. *(Pause.)*

TONY. Do you and Ann have sex a lot?

BRIAN. I'm not sure I want to get into that … said the Bishop to the Chorus Girl … *(Pause.)* Now there's a grand old tradition gone.

TONY. Which?

BRIAN. The "Chorus Girl." I mean the kind they used to have. Third from the left and no discernible talent. *(Pause.)* No, Ann and I don't have a whole lot of sex now because, quite frankly, we became exhausted. I mean, we spent nearly three years frantically going through the Kama Sutra trying to conceive *something*, even a child perhaps. And doctors kept telling us to do this and do that, and we'd set our calendars and our watches. We'd race home at all hours to try the latest theory. One of the biggest problems was the giggles. We'd get into these strange configurations and start laughing helplessly. Hopelessly. Well, it's hard to … sustain … while laughing. So now we watch a lot of cable TV. *(Pause.)* When we first met, Ann was very difficult. She made me wear one of those penile Macintoshes because she was sure I'd had a past, or was having a present. Safe Sex had just begun its grim progress. Ironically, I got a clean bill of health and …

TONY. I thought you didn't want to talk about this.

BRIAN. You brought it up. How about you and Joy? No, don't tell me. It'll depress me. How's the book design business?

TONY. You know, most people don't even know books are "designed"?

BRIAN. Everything is designed. It's a shame, really. A chair, a piece of paper. *(Pause.)* "But only God can make a tree." *(He begins to laugh quietly.)*

TONY. Here comes Annie.

BRIAN. Annie could probably make a tree. *(Ann enters.)*

ANN. I think I know what has to happen. I think I have to check with Charlie Russell who's with us and who does wills and estates and stuff. I'm not sure this is strictly kosher.

BRIAN. What you're doing?

ANN. What Mom's doing. I think Dad left us as secondary beneficiaries and …

BRIAN. Well, yes, there's always that solution; you could kill her.

ANN. Brian, I am trying to be serious here. Of course, you're so unconcerned. But I always found it a little suspicious that you proposed marriage to me right after you first set eyes on this place.

BRIAN. That is a complete fiction.

ANN. It is not. It is a fact. You know I do not forget things like that. We came out here, I introduced you to Mom and Dad —

BRIAN. Which rather led me to assume you were in the marrying mode,

ANN. Assume away. The fact is, you came out here for the day — it was a summer day like this one, it was July, the twenty-fourth in fact, and afterwards we went to Healey's for a beer. And at 10:35 P.M., you asked me to marry you.

TONY. Is Healey's still there?

28

BRIAN. Look, I don't pretend that I'm not disappointed. But disappointment is one thing; intrigue and ... yes, avarice are quite another.

ANN. Avarice!? It's not the money I want, Bri. It's not the ... the "real estate," if you will. It's "the place." This is the place we grew up in.

BRIAN. "And now they're cutting down my beautiful cherry orchard."

ANN. Well, don't think they won't!

BRIAN. You don't have a cherry orchard.

ANN. No, but we have a lot of trees and bushes and ... and *things* that Dad put in here and that developers will remove. Because that's exactly what will happen. Some developer will come in here and rename it Windsor Chase or something ...

BRIAN. No, no, no. Some rich retiree, just as bored as Marjorie is bored, will buy the place and make a few minor alterations ... you know, a gazebo here and there, or whatever, and that will be it. And years from now we'll drive by with our daughter and say, "Look, Ursula, that used to be your grandfather's house." And Ursula will say, "Can we go to McDonald's?" And that is the way the world turns, Ann.

ANN. Ursula?

BRIAN. Just teasing. But the rest is accurate.

TONY. I don't get it, Annie.

ANN What?

TONY. Why you care so much.

ANN. I care about a lot of things. I don't wear all my hearts on my sleeve like you do, Tony, but I care.

TONY. But that's just it. You already have so much to care about. Why do you want more?

ANN. Tony: All these things I do ... have done ... all these "accomplishments" — were for Dad. They were what Dad expected of me. Told me he did. I remember even when he died, that day in the hospital ...

TONY. I wasn't there. No one seemed to have noticed.

ANN. That is not true. We were scrambling, Tony. As I've told you a thousand times. Mom called me in a panic. She ... didn't know where she was, who she'd called. She called the cleaners first!

By mistake. Well, you know she's always sending stuff out to them ... Anyway. Dad was lying there looking like a little boy ... hospitals do that; make you look like a child ... and he knocked something over. One of those "bendy" straws they give you. So, mother starts to lean over to get it, and Dad says, "No. Annie'll do that ... Annie'll take care of it." And then he kinda closed his eyes for a minute, and then *we* had heart attacks, of course, and then he looked at me and he said "Lots to do ... Lots to do ... " They tell me he didn't really know where he was or anything. But Christ, he's been telling me that ever since I can remember. Ever since college. Ever since high school. And I loved it. *(Pause.)* I loved him. Oh my god, I loved Daddy. And I miss him so damn much! ... *(Recovering.)* But now I've lots to do for me. My stuff. Ann's stuff. *(Pause.)* Ann's family.

TONY. Ann called me five minutes after he died. It was quick, you know.

BRIAN. We had been trying to find you, Tony.

ANN. I must've called your office ten times, and Joy was —

TONY. I know. *(Pause.)* I was at the movies.

ANN. What?!

TONY. That's why no one could find me. I was at a movie.

ANN. In the middle of the afternoon?

TONY. *(Belligerent.)* So?

BRIAN. What was it?

TONY. I don't remember.

BRIAN. Of course you remember. What was it? *(Sound: A car driving in.)*

ANN. Who's that?

TONY. *(Happy to change the subject.)* Probably Palestrina. You've got to talk to him, Ann. He's just ripping mother off with this service contract scam.

ANN. No, it's not him. Oh my god. It's Perry. Will Perry. The real estate agent.

BRIAN. The wheels of destiny are clicking right along.

TONY. Is he alone? Does he have *buyers?!*

ANN. No. He's going up to the house. C'mon, Tony. We can't let mother sign anything.

TONY. You go, Annie. I never know what to say.

ANN. You, get off your ass and come with me! People like Will Perry don't take women seriously. *(To Brian.)* One of Dad's golf buddies. You don't have to say anything, Tony. Just stand there and be male.

TONY. All right.

BRIAN. Be sure you've got your penis.

ANN. *(To Brian.)* And you stay here.

BRIAN. Oh yes. Two hysterical women, one silent male and some British fag, that would never do. I'll just sit here and enjoy the final moments of the Reich.

TONY. Don't say that. Don't even think that.

ANN. Come on! *(Ann leaves hurriedly. Tony follows, then turns back to Brian.)*

TONY. *Jurassic Park.*

BRIAN. I beg your pardon?

TONY. That was the movie. *(He starts off stops.) The Sequel. (He exits.)*

BRIAN. Bloody Yanks. *(He pours himself a drink.)* Their turn to lose the Empire. *(Brian walks over to gaze at the pool and raises his glass in a toast.)* Here's to American moisture. To swimming pools and showers. Sprinklers and water-beds. Jacuzzis and iced tea. When in doubt, add water. If Debussy had owned a swimming pool, would he have written *La Mer*? ... One wonders. *(Joy enters, unseen by Brian.)*

JOY. Hello. *(Brian turns to see her.)*

BRIAN. Joy! Like the answer to a prayer.

JOY. They're all being terribly polite and desperate in there. Very McDermott. I got out before the "you-know-what" hits the fan. *(She walks over to look at the pool.)* I think it's greener.

BRIAN. They're an odd group, aren't they? *(Joy does not reply.)* We've been married to the McDermotts for ... well, Ann and I for four years; you and Tony longer ... and we've never had a chance to commiserate, you and I.

JOY. Is that the word? "Commiserate"?

BRIAN. Or evaluate. Whatever.

JOY. I have nothing to say, really. That you don't already know. Two children. Tony.

BRIAN. Three children.

JOY. Yes, perhaps. *(Pause.)* And you?

BRIAN. No children. Ann.

JOY. No children. But one soon.

BRIAN. I suppose so. I wish, though ... I wish she weren't doing it as a sort of debating move. Proposition: That the American woman can excel professionally and also be a supermom. Oh, the child will be ... good for us, I suppose. If only it had been the result of passion rather than polemic. Poor little thing. Its every move will be charted and assessed. It will be reared by professionals with the highest credentials, instead of by sweet Ann, or by some loony relation, as I was: a mad Cornish grandmother who went against every rule of child psychology. Taught me to be afraid of everything, convinced me of ghosts and a wrathful God actively planning my Eternal Damnation. Told me there were mermaids, and mer*men,* and Willies and hobgoblins, and took me to Merlin's cave at Tintagel ... scared the life into me. Made me, for better or for worse, complicated and unpredictable. Even interesting at the odd moment. If one has nothing better to do. But our child will probably be protected from such medieval circumstance. *(Pause.)* How do you raise your kids? They are quite beguiling, you know.

JOY. I don't know how I raise them. I raise them. I punish them when they're bad and praise them when they're good. I'm sure I also punish them when I'm tired, and Tony praises them far too much. But that's for them to sort out, I think. And I think you underestimate Ann.

BRIAN. Well, we'll all have a lot of rules, that's for sure. She doesn't drink, doesn't smoke, no red meat, no sugar, no — "commercial TV," no suntan, no fur, no ivory, no wood — unless absolutely essential, but then no plastic either because it refuses to biodegrade. She is the standard bearer of the "No" generation, a wonderful group who go through life abstaining from everything.

JOY. Yes, Tony has a lot of that, too. But his "noes" and "nons" change weekly.

BRIAN. Do you suppose it finally ends up — the "no" person — in a dark room with *no* electrical or solar radiation — and *no* clothing, and nothing but distilled water and soya beans? Having finally attained what? "No-ness"?

JOY. And being very sure everyone else is impressed.

BRIAN. And being sure everyone else is *very* impressed. *(Pause.)*

JOY. What you want to ask me, of course, is why I married him.

BRIAN. Not my business, is it?

JOY. I was dancing, you see. Really dancing, in those days. Not the show dancing I did later to pay the bills.

BRIAN. Oh, but that was exciting! Broadway musicals. Most impressive.

JOY. *(Ignoring that.)* I was dancing. We had a small group called ... Excelsior ... and Tony, who was just out of college too, sort of hung around and then designed our sets and costumes. And they were good. They were really good. He had a flair for that. So you see, we were all ... creating stuff together. I fell in love dancing. *(Pause.)* Tony misses all that. Everything since then has been ... difficult.

BRIAN. What will you do about all this? This Marjorie business?

JOY. Breathe a great sigh of relief.

BRIAN. Has she been a "mother-in-law"?

JOY. I like Marjorie well enough. But there has been so very much of her and Jack — even from the grave, Jack — that there hasn't been a whole lot of Tony.

BRIAN. I see.

JOY. It's terrible having a father as successful as Jack was. Bad enough he was a top executive, but then the songwriting thing.

BRIAN. Just the one song, really. A fluke.

JOY. That's all you need when it's a standard. sometimes I'll be in the check-out line at the supermarket and I'll hear it on the Muzak — "Many Happy Returns" — I'll hear that and I'll think: I wonder how many times a day Tony hears that. Everything was so easy for Jack. Everything is so difficult for Tony.

BRIAN. Everything is so difficult for Ann. Because if it's not, she finds something that is. *(Pause.)*

JOY. I get up in the morning and get the kids dressed and fed, and get Tony ... well, fed, and drive the kids to school and Tony to the train. Then I do a few errands and go to quiet home. Where I put on Tchaikovsky or Delibes and my tights and leotard, and dance for hours on end. Dance till I drop. Then I shower and put on my sensible clothes, pick up my sensible children, and later my exhausted husband. He's always exhausted. What can they do in

Manhattan that they come home so exhausted, say I who have danced all day. *(Pause.)*

BRIAN. You know ... just by way of giving us food for thought in a dry season ... I've often wondered if you and I could have an affair.

JOY. No! Never! Definitely not! Don't even think of such a thing. How could you *think* of such a thing!?

BRIAN. Ah, so there *is* hope.

JOY. *(Starting to leave.)* Good-bye, Brian.

BRIAN. I absolutely adore you.

JOY. I didn't hear that.

BRIAN. I do. I love you. I "lust after you in my heart" — an American thing to do.

JOY. "Thou shalt not covet thy brother-in-law's wife." Even for a minute. Thou shalt not.

BRIAN. But I do.

JOY. Well, that's too bad.

BRIAN. But what shall we do about it?

JOY. Not a damned thing. First of all, it shows a total lack of respect — never mind love — for Ann. And that disgusts me ... Secondly, it shows that you think I'm some sort of child ... a little Asian kewpie doll ... Madam Butterfly or Miss Saigon!

BRIAN. No. I think you are a woman. A divinely, womanly woman, who —

JOY. And you are so typically, boringly male.

BRIAN. What?!

JOY. The male sex! Sticking out there; trying to push its way into everything. I know ... I've got a little boy.

BRIAN. Oh, well, yes, the yin and yang and so on, but that's the fun of it, isn't it?

JOY. The fun of it is that I'm going to tell Ann all about this.

BRIAN. Oh my god. Why?

JOY. Because you men always expect to get away with bullshit like this. And because maybe then I'll be rid of the whole bunch of you.

BRIAN. Then you *don't* really love Tony! I knew it.

JOY. Oh Brian, grow up. *(Tony has entered. Joy sees him and Brian sees her shocked expression. He wheels around and sees Tony also.)*

TONY. *(Pale and shaken.)* I can't believe this is happening ...

BRIAN. Now, Tony …

TONY. Just when you think you've got everything all figured out …

BRIAN. Tony, you mustn't make too much of this …

JOY. Why not?

TONY. I was just standing there, listening to them talk about the house … and I don't know what came over me. You know that porcelain horse and rider Mom and Dad got in Budapest?

BRIAN. *(Totally confused.)* What? …

TONY. I just threw it at Will Perry.

JOY. Oh, Tony … You promised …

TONY. *(Sitting …)* Is this happening?

ANN. *(Offstage.)* Tony!!!!

TONY. *(Getting up.)* This is happening. Ann's furious. *(Joy storms off toward the rose garden.)* Joy's furious … The pool's looking great! *(Tony exits toward the pool — Ann enters.)*

ANN. Tony …

BRIAN. Is Will Perry all right?

ANN. He's bleeding. And shaking and muttering. Maybe a stroke, I don't know.

BRIAN. Oh for Christ's sake. Has anyone called a doctor?

ANN. I did. An ambulance is on the way. Mom's running back and forth with towels and things. It's a mess.

BRIAN. What can I do?

ANN. Just get Tony out of here. Perry's going to press charges of course. Why shouldn't he? We'll get a lawyer for Tony, but for now just get him out of here. I think he's 'round the bend.

BRIAN. I think your whole family's "'round the bend," that's what I think.

ANN. Brian, I don't much care what you think. *(The sound of approaching siren.)* Oh swell, theatrics and everything. Brian, just do this little thing, will you?

BRIAN. Christ. *(Tony strolls in.)*

ANN. Tony? What *are* you doing? *(The siren is getting louder.)*

TONY. Look, it's almost blue. The water. Isn't that great? I'm really sorry I did that, Ann. *(Siren stops as the ambulance is heard pulling in.)* Maybe we'd better give them a hand, huh?

BRIAN. That won't be necessary, Tony. Leave it to the professionals. Let's you and I go somewhere for a drink. Healey's.

TONY. Is Healey's still there?

BRIAN. I'm sure it is.

TONY. Great, sounds good. I don't drink anymore, though.

BRIAN. Maybe just this once.

TONY. Maybe just this once. *(The two men start out.)* Where's Joy?

BRIAN. She's taking a walk. She went for a walk.

TONY. Oh good. I'm so glad. Ann, if the pool people call, will you talk with them? Tell them they've really got to ...

ANN. Yes!! Get out!

TONY. Right. Yeah. *Good* idea. *(Brian and Tony exit. Ann goes to drink table. She looks at the gin bottle, then pours herself a straight shot and downs it in one swallow. Blackout.)*

SCENE THREE

Lights up on Marjorie and Ann. Marjorie is looking at the pool.

MARJORIE. What a revolting smell ... Wouldn't it be nice if Tony were five years old again and I could just send him to his room for the summer.

ANN. Dad used to do that. But you'd let him out.

MARJORIE. Now, apparently, he wants back in. *(She comes back towards Ann.)* Those ambulance people made a perfect mess of the living room. And of course Tony had to pick the one piece of crockery that's irreplaceable. All the men are gone, thank God?

ANN. All gone.

MARJORIE *(Looking off beyond, pool.)* Look ... beyond the rose garden; on the old lawn ... there's Joy. Dancing ... naked as a babe. *(Ann looks off R. She laughs softly. Marjorie goes to her chair.)* My, what a day this has become.

ANN. It has become the most important day in our lives. And is beginning to fray at the edges, I think.

MARJORIE. And yet if I were dying, suddenly died one morning, there would not be all this: breaking things and storming about and ... well, dancing for some. No. It hasn't got to do with me. It's The Place. We've always called it that, haven't we? "The Place." What we are dealing with here is a loss of "place."

ANN. Conservancy. My specialty, don't forget. I save the trees and the oceans, the wetlands and deserts and creatures great and small that creep upon the earth. But there are personal conservancies as well. This ... yes, "place" has been our center. Just the having it here is important. We're selling off everything these days. The lots get smaller and smaller. Each subdivision diminishes.

MARJORIE. Do these things really concern you?

ANN. Mother. What a question!

MARJORIE. I have always assumed that you did these things — fought these good fights — to impress people. As you did everything else: the ballet classes and horse shows, the Phi Beta key, Harvard Law School — yes, even marrying an Englishman, all these things seemed more for public display than anything ... wanted. Even this child business —

ANN. Yes, I know: "Abrasive Annie." Brian says my whole life revolves around "getting" people. Proving them wrong. Well I do enjoy that as a matter of fact. And I don't mind if I make an impression. Is that so wrong? Putting my imprint?

MARJORIE. You go through life as if you're trying to win an argument.

ANN. And I will.

MARJORIE. Whereas Tony —

ANN. — is broke. Plain and simple. He'll be let go soon at the publishing house.

MARJORIE. What?!

ANN. Joy told me two months ago. She'll have to get a job ... (Looking off R.) ... unless she's gone 'round the bend. Brian says we've all gone "'round the bend."

MARJORIE. I'd love to go 'round the bend. And see what's there. It's the straight and narrow that kills you. Before you die. But Tony. Oh, Tony. How could he be so ... ineffectual. And what would he do here? Paint pictures and annoy my swimming pool? And Joy living like a poor relation, while grandmother takes care of the brood? No. I won't have it.

ANN. Grandmothers are supposed to dote on their grandchildren.
MARJORIE. In their dotage, yes. I love my grandchildren. At a distance and from time to time. But I've done all that. I spent decades caring for … and *driving* people: you and Tony to classes and camp, to pediatricians and orthodontists, Jack to trains and planes, the dogs to kennel and myself to distraction. These treads are very worn, Ann. Added to which, I was never greatly blessed with the maternal instinct. Nor were you.
ANN. As unthinkable as this may be, mother, you might be wrong.
MARJORIE. You don't need a child.
ANN. But I want one. I want a son I can name Jack, let run around here and climb these big old trees, and have a place he can call "The Place." And yes, someday maybe even live here. Tend these gardens and worry about the pool and the roof. Or even just to summer here. A few weeks of the year. This place. His place. Jack's place. *(Pause. Marjorie remains still.)*
MARJORIE. Direct hit.
ANN. What?
MARJORIE. You have scored a direct hit. The old lady's listing and limping to port. Is this how you "get" people? Even your poor old Mum?
ANN. What do you mean?
MARJORIE. I mean I was fine — not McDermott "fine," but really fine. I had it all planned: Off to foreign shores and a new life and let the old world sort itself out without me. When Jack left, the world was open to me, as he would wish it to be. Then you come here with a sort of *Readers Digest* picture of a barefoot boy climbing trees and you name him Jack and suddenly I've got responsibilities again. There is "The Place" and something to be tended. It's most unfair.
ANN. But, Mom, you can still go places. New Zealand or wherever. Around the world.
MARJORIE. The world teems with traveling widows, Ann. Consulting timetables, worrying over tips and hurrying to museums before they close. No, I wanted more than that. But it's selfish, I suppose. Dear god, why can't one simply … discard. *(Pause. The sky is getting darker.)* One day during that last week when I sat

with Jack at the hospital, he said — out of the blue — "Be sure to have that sumac cut down and taken out. They're just overgrown weeds, that's all they are" ... And look. I've never done it. *(Joy walks on, dressed as before. She stops.)*
JOY. Oh. You're here. I heard the sirens and thought ... I thought everyone had gone. And I didn't want to find out why. *(Joy crosses to L. stops.)* I have to tell you something, Ann. Though it's not really very important. *(Joy exits, L.)*
ANN. *(Wearily.)* Oh dear. Brian must have made a pass at her.
MARJORIE. What?!
ANN. Oh, everyone. His fatal weakness. If it gets to be a problem, I suppose I'll leave him to his devices. That's the other reason I want ... my Jack. *(She starts off L.)* I'd better tell her all about Tony and the flying ceramics. We can go to Healey's Bar together and ... what? ... be wifely with our men. Draw the wagons into a circle ... Conservancy. Poor Joy. *(Ann exits, L. Marjorie sits still for a long time ... Far off, a rumbling of thunder is heard.)*
MARJORIE. There. Thunder in the hills, Jack. *(Another rumble of thunder is heard.)* Just when I'd gotten my planet in order. Was it wrong of me, Jack, to just ... cast away? *(A man appears, in a bathing suit and wearing flippers on his feet. He has a diving mask and snorkel at rest on the top of this head. He is in his 60's, silver-haired and athletic. Marjorie, though clearly aware of his presence, does not look at him. He is expected.)*
MAN. Nothing wrong, old girl. Everything right as rain ...
MARJORIE. We might get some, too.
MAN. Tony's damned chemicals stinking up the place.
MARJORIE. I know. *(He comes down next to Marjorie and puts his hand on her shoulder. She pats it gently.)* Here's my man. Come from the sea.
MAN. No chlorine in the sea, old girl.
MARJORIE. Come from the suburban Connecticut sea, my grizzly old Fisher King. *(The Man laughs.)* What shall I do with them?
MAN. Hmm?
MARJORIE. With our dreadful children, Jack?
MAN. You said it. Not me. Well, you say everything here, don't you.
MARJORIE. Is it all me? Nothing of you at all?

MAN. A soggy memory, m'love. A great beached fish.

MARJORIE. Or is it me who's dreadful?

MAN. Can't cut loose.

MARJORIE. But I must.

MAN. Them, I mean. They can't cut loose.

MARJORIE. "Blest be the ties that bind" …

MAN. Good tune, that. Bullshit, of course, but catchy. Just like most of my stuff.

MARJORIE. You could write songs. That's still amazing to me.

MAN. Oh hell, lady mine, I don't know if I did write them.

MARJORIE. Of course you did.

MAN. They came to me. But I always had this nagging concern … nags me in my grave … that I'd heard those tunes before. Especially the big one — "Many Happy Returns." I'll swear I heard that tune when I was a kid.

MARJORIE. No one ever contested it.

MAN. Oh hell no. Hard case to make. The point is: Mine was a negligible talent.

MARJORIE. Jack!

MAN. You know it. Hell, you're thinking it. Nothing I say but what you're thinking.

MARJORIE. Nevertheless … you were a keen man of business. Tony can do nothing. *Nothing.* Not an artist, not a merchant, not even a rude mechanical. Your shadow is too strong.

MAN. More bullshit. I didn't do well; I *married* well.

MARJORIE. Please don't say that.

MAN. Your script. You know it. I married Marjorie Tate and Daddy Tate set me up.

MARJORIE. You *never* worked for my father!

MAN. Didn't have to. The Old Boy network, my love. I worked for his friends. I didn't have to sell car insurance at some regional office, did I?

MARJORIE. That wasn't your line. Finance was your strength.

MAN. They taught me how to make a buck in the privacy of the back office, yes. I accomplished nothing. Favoritism and patronage and privileged information. The right name and club. Still, it gave me a lot of spare cash. And spare time.

MARJORIE. And you used it well. Turned it into music.

MAN. Sure. Paid off a few people. Publishers and deejays.

MARJORIE. I don't want to hear this.

MAN. You never did. You never would. I was always glad to know you had that little weakness.

MARJORIE. Weakness?

MAN. The things you chose not to know. Besides, who needs to?

MARJORIE. *(Decisively.)* Tony.

MAN. What?!

MARJORIE. Tony *needs* to know.

MAN. Oh come on, old girl. Keep the myth alive.

MARJORIE. Why? *(Pause.)*

MAN. You still haven't taken out that sumac. Bloody weed!

MARJORIE. Don't change the subject.

MAN. Your script.

MARJORIE. If I leave here ... will you come with?

MAN. No, lady. Here's my earth.

MARJORIE. Yes?...

MAN. So you see — it's really up to you. I am ... at your disposal.

MARJORIE. Oh, Jack ...

MAN. Drain the pool. Send the old man down the drain.

MARJORIE. Surely there's some life for you. It doesn't really end?

MAN. Marjorie. We have successfully avoided religion all our lives ... let's not cave in now. Besides, in my case it would be redundant.

MARJORIE. Nothing then?

MAN. Oh, a grand tonic chord. A terrific sense of completion, and the muscles ease ... and no melancholy ever after.

MARJORIE. I have "immortal longings" in me, Jack.

MAN. Try New Zealand. *(Starts to sing and dance like an old vaudevillian.)*

"You'll never know
    If you haven't tried.
    Double your money
    If not satisfied
    I'm your guaranteed lover
    With a lifetime guaranteeeeee!"
That one never caught on.

MARJORIE. Don't you make fun of me.

41

MAN. Hey. I can't do anything that doesn't come from you. Which is even better than "I can't give you anything but love, baby." God, I loved Fats Waller. I had none of that ... joy.

MARJORIE. Joy.

MAN. She's a grand girl. Let her go, too. She will. She knows what's good for her. Don't give her safe haven here. Throw 'em all out. The whole brood.

MARJORIE. But Jack. I mean ... "to Grandmother's house we *go.*"

MAN. And, "my what big teeth you have!"

MARJORIE. Ann wants to have a son. Wants to call him "Jack."

MAN. Better call him John. Find out if he's a "Jack."

MARJORIE. I should be here for that. And "The Place" should be here.

MAN. Why? Did you ever go back to your father's place? Now *there* was a *place!*

MARJORIE. He sold it.

MAN. Had to. That "unpleasantness" with the Department of Internal Revenue. Ah, well ... *(Sings.)*
   "I spent all of my time livin' it up,
      How'm I gonna live it down?"
That could've made it on the country charts. I put it in the wrong market.

MARJORIE. All these distractions ...

MAN. Your stream of consciousness, not mine. *(Sings.)*
   "Row, row, row your boat,
      Gently down the stream ... "

MARJORIE. Oh, it's all so easy for you!

MAN. Death ought to have some advantages. *(Sings.)*
   "Wish me when I put to sea,
      Many happy returns ... "

MARJORIE. Jack. *(She starts to cry.)* ... Oh, Jack ... *(Offstage: the sound of a car driving in.)*

MAN. Oh dear.

MARJORIE. Don't leave! Don't you dare leave me.

MAN. Can't leave. *(He sits.)* ... Not *here. (Tony enters, L.)*

TONY. Mother ...

MARJORIE. Hello, dear.

TONY. Mother, I am terribly, terribly ... sorry.

MARJORIE. Yes … Well …
TONY. Pool looks good.
MARJORIE. What?!
TONY. I don't know what happened, really …
MARJORIE. You seriously injured an old and esteemed friend of the family, is what happened.
TONY. I was standing there listening to Ann and Mr. Perry jabbering on and on — all that kind of talk I never really understand — legalisms, finances … things — and I saw everything ending. Like when you're reading a great book and you suddenly realize the author's beginning to wind things up. I panicked.
MARJORIE. Will was simply trying to explain, as clearly as possible, the difficulty of maintaining a place like this in this day and —
TONY. I'm especially sorry because this really holds up your New Zealand trip. You deserve a holiday.
MARJORIE. Holiday?
TONY. But we're all going to have to stick together now.
MARJORIE. What do you mean? Whatever do you mean?
MAN. I know.
TONY. Well, Mother, this thing's going to go to court unless we settle with Will Perry. Or if it does go to court, I mean, we'll need Charlie Sylvester …
MAN. Oh, Christ.
TONY. … and I can't afford that kind of expense. But if you ask him, I mean, Charlie and Dad. You know …
MAN. Charlie Sylvester is a prick.
TONY. He'll probably give me a break. (Pause.) Mom?
MARJORIE. Charlie lost Madge last year … I loved Madge.
TONY. Mom? I mean I'm not going to jail, for Christ's sake!
MARJORIE. Why not?
TONY. What?!
MARJORIE. You deliberately injured one of your father's and my dearest friends …
MAN. Will Perry's a prick, too. All my friends are pricks.
MARJORIE. … and you ought to pay for it.
TONY. Oh come on!
MARJORIE. In the old days your father would have punished

43

you; now perhaps the state of Connecticut has to.

TONY. Mother, I am not going to *jail*. Do you know what happens to people — to young men — in jail?

MAN. He's being melodramatic. A few days in the county cooler, a stiff fine and probation.

MARJORIE. There will be a stiff fine, you know. Can you pay it?

TONY. Of course I can't pay it. I don't have any money.

MARJORIE. Well, why *not?*

TONY. I'm an *artist!*

MAN. And I'm Beethoven. *(Marjorie laughs.)*

TONY. What's so damn funny?

MARJORIE. Nothing. Sorry.

TONY. Look. I said I'm sorry. I don't know … Joy and Ann came to Healey's. Ann started talking the way she does, about this strategy and that strategy. Joy didn't say a word. She just sat there looking at the table. I couldn't stand it.

MARJORIE. So you ran away.

TONY. I came here.

MARJORIE. You always come here.

TONY. Yes? Does that mean I shouldn't?

MARJORIE. No, I didn't mean —

TONY. Yes you did. Yes I think really you did. *(He walks over to R., looks at the pool.)*

MAN. *(To Marjorie.)* Will Perry'll settle out of court. The real estate market's lousy —

TONY. I don't know why I come back. Lots of us are doing that.

MARJORIE. Us?"

TONY. My friends. My generation. Going back to home towns. Going back to school. Just going back. 'Cause there's nothing else.

MARJORIE. Nonsense.

TONY. No. It's true. It's all been done. The agenda. Brave New World. Pushed to the sea both East and West. People go to California and jump off the Golden Gate Bridge or O.D. on drugs. Or they go home, "Uncle!" … "I give!" … "King's X" … Just let me come home, Mom. I can't do anything. We'll help out. Joy is great at everything. The kids are good. They really are. We'll do everything for you. You can … you can just *bask*. In the sun.

MARJORIE. And January? February?

44

MAN. Tell him to wipe his nose and get out of here.

TONY. Mom I can't do it. I can't make it. There's nothing to make. I do the New York thing, the commute thing. I do lunch and all that other crap, and my mind isn't even there. I'm somewhere else. I don't know what people are saying to me half the time. When I left the School of Design, I had a kind of vague agenda. But there's nothing there. There are thousands of designers. Who gives a shit? Who gives a good goddamn about *design* when we're all just treading water. Nothing's happening. The street is jammed with people running every which way. And nothing's happening. Nothing at all. I am such a disappointment to you. I know that. God, it's terrible to know that. *(He sits. Pause.)*

MAN. You might as well face it, old girl. You're stuck with him.

MARJORIE. Really?

TONY. Yes, really.

MARJORIE. Mmm? *(She realizes Tony has not heard the Man.)* Oh.

TONY. I mean if it were just me. But it's Joy and the kids. Oh, don't worry. I'll get out of this. It's a ... a slump.

MAN. Sure.

TONY. I need a year ... or two ... just to paint. I've got to get back to basics. To my art.

MAN. Oh, Jesus.

TONY. Then everything will be fine. I'm *(Pause.)* fine.

MARJORIE. You are?

TONY. Yeah. I'm beginning to see it now. We'll clean up all this ... Will Perry mess ... and then Joy and I will come here — just for a while. A year. Maybe year and a half. I'll get out the old easel and set myself up in the shed like I used to do in summer ... And then I'll be ready to take another crack.

MARJORIE. At what?

TONY. Things. The big bad world.

MARJORIE. I see.

TONY. Look, that pool is positively blue. Like the Grotto at Capri. Can I make you a drink, Mom? Oh my god — Joy!

MARJORIE. Yes?

TONY. Well, I just left her there at Healey's. We've got to get back home. Mrs. Lopez hates it when we're late and she's the kids' favorite. Mom, I'm really sorry. Really. Believe me. If you can just call Charlie Sylvester and sort of warn him. Then I'll give him a ring the minute anyone makes a move on me. If Will Perry thinks he can scare the McDermotts ... well, "United We Stand," right?

MARJORIE. Tony ...

TONY. Don't even think about it. I don't want you even to think about it. What did Dad used to say? "Just keep the garden growing; let me go off to the wars!"

MAN. Never said that in my life.

MARJORIE. Tony, I must talk to you.

TONY. Not now, Mom. Got Joy and a babysitter waiting. I'll phone tomorrow.

MARJORIE. It's about your father.

TONY. Dad?

MARJORIE. Yes, you see, Tony ... and I've never really ... *dealt* with this before, but ... *(This is very hard for Marjorie.)* I told you — I've always told you — that this place and Jack's success, that those were examples of what a person can do with their lives if they ... And Jack was a wonderful fellow. Wonderful. But, honey, like most every other "self-made man" you'll meet in this world, he did it with someone else's money. In Jack's case: mine. And my father's connections. There. *(Pause. Tony does not seem to react.)* Oh, I know what you're thinking: the songs, the music. Yes, he had a flair for that ... but he also had the money to buy their success. And that's what he did. Jack could charm people. And, Jack could write a check. I've never said those things out loud before ... *(Looking at Jack.)* ... but I've thought them.

TONY. How dare you!

MARJORIE. What?!

TONY. How dare you say those things about my father. About your husband! I refuse to listen to any of this.

MARJORIE. But you *should.*

TONY. My God, I knew you'd been saying some weird things lately, and getting morbid out here, all alone, but *this.* I'll just forget I heard any of this, okay?

MARJORIE. Tony! I am only trying to help you. Trying to get you out from under this god-like figure you've invented, this ... Jack.

TONY. Help me?! You're not helping me! You're ... — I'm going now. I'm going back to Healey's, and I won't tell Joy a word about all this. I'll just try to forget that ... *(He has almost left, then turns back.)* "Help me?"?! Christ, Mother ... he was my last *excuse! (He exits, L.)*

MAN. You see what happens, old girl? Dependency has an amazing capacity to regenerate itself. And, hell, it's what we want, isn't it?

MARJORIE. What?

MAN. To have people depend on us?

MARJORIE. Why do I?

MAN. Oh hell, lady, I don't know *why.* "Why" is Freud or philosophy or something. I just know that's the way it shakes out. You put in all this — a house and garden, care and protection, education and trust fund — you do all that, and you've got 'em. You've bound them to you for life. Only one way out.

MARJORIE. Your way?

MAN. And even then ... look at me. Still lingering on a summer afternoon.

MARJORIE. How do I break it?

MAN. Don't want to.

MARJORIE. Yes, I do.

MAN. Naw, you want us: Ann, Tony ... me. You leave this place and it all goes.

MARJORIE. Yes?

MAN. Yes. *(Pause.)*

MARJORIE. Promise?

MAN. What's that supposed to mean?

MARJORIE. How dare you!

MAN. *(Starting to leave.)* Getting dark. Time for a dip.

MARJORIE. You tell me your life was negligible, which means, of course, that mine was too, I suppose. You tell me I've got these dependents forever, as if ... as if any kind of individual choices were denied. A sort of patio-and-pool Calvinism!

MAN. The point is, old girl: It's not this place you want to leave. It's this life. It's the goddamn pool and the goddamn grocery lists, and the goddamn gardeners and the goddamn Sunday nights doing the double-crostic in front of Masterpiece Theatre. And do you know what you'll find in New Zealand? A goddamn pool, the goddamn grocery lists, the goddamn gardeners and the goddamn Sunday nights doing the London *Times* crossword in front of the

47

"telly." Now, that's a fact, so my advice, my real advice is: Just forget it. Do as I did. *(Pause.)* Relax. *(The sound of a car driving into the driveway.)* Oh no ... Now it's the other one.

MARJORIE. That's what you did? You just relaxed?

MAN. Exactly. All the easy strategies. All the simplest tunes.

MARJORIE. I suppose we did ... how awful to realize...

MAN. Don't let them catch you talking to yourself ... They'd love a chance to have you committed. *(Brian enters, rumpled.)*

MARJORIE. I never do when they're ... *(Sees Brian.)*

BRIAN. I talk to myself, too. Really the only person whose opinions interest me.

MARJORIE. *(Sharply.)* What are you doing here? *(Ann enters.)*

ANN. Will you please take him, Mother?

MARJORIE. What?

BRIAN. I'm being sent down. I've been naughty, you see, and I'm being sent down.

ANN. I won't have him in my apartment.

BRIAN. Our apartment.

ANN. Bernstein Realty's apartment.

MARJORIE. What am I supposed to do with him?

ANN. Put him in a back room and let him grow up.

MARJORIE. Dear Brian, were you being virile again with Joy?

BRIAN. Oh I suppose so ... why all the fuss? *(Brian picks up the book that's been on the table all day.)* Kierkegaard?! Oh, well, that explains everything ...

MAN. *(Referring to Brian.)* You know, actually I like *him.*

MARJORIE. *(To Man.)* Kierkegaard?

BRIAN. Yes.

MAN. No. Brian. I never read Kierke-whoever.

MARJORIE. Ann, I hardly think it's fair to dump your marital problems on my verandah. If he's been bad, deal with it. *(Brian starts to pour himself a drink.)*

BRIAN. Thanks, I will.

ANN. You've had enough.

BRIAN. Never. Never enough ... *(He puts down bottle.)* Oh, alright. *(He stretches out on the recliner.)* Good night all. You can decide what to do with the body in the morning ... *(He dozes off.)*

MARJORIE. Well, that absolutely does it

ANN. He can be a pig sometimes, can't he?

MARJORIE. Not him. You.

ANN. Me?

MAN. *(Singing softly.)* "Bid me, when I go to sea ... "

MARJORIE. Dropping off your sick puppy for me to tend. Just assuming —

ANN. Oh, mother, I just want to scare him. Teach him a lesson.

MAN. *(Still singing ...)* "Many happy returns ... "

MARJORIE. And I am the object ... the pillory you employ.

ANN. No, it's just —

MARJORIE. And if I were not here? If "The Place" were not here?

MAN. But it is, you see.

ANN. Let's not get into this tonight. I'm acting on impulse, okay? It's something I'm trying. I don't analyze anymore.

BRIAN. ... doesn't drink, doesn't analyze ...

ANN. Go to sleep.

MARJORIE. Ann, I have come to a ... decision. About this. About all of this.

ANN. We know. You're going to New Zealand.

MARJORIE. No. I am not.

MAN. *(Starting to leave.)* So long, old girl ...

ANN. Mother ... Are you alright?

MARJORIE. Never better. And *not* going to New Zealand.

ANN. Well, thank God. The day hasn't been a complete loss.

MARJORIE. I'm going somewhere far more culturally remote and challenging, where civilization struggles day by day.

ANN. Mother ...

MARJORIE. I'm going to Manhattan.

ANN. What?!

MARJORIE. I'm going to take a place in deepest Manhattan.

MAN. Good-bye, old girl.

ANN. Whatever for?

MAN. You've left me.

MARJORIE. For my life. For my sanity. For something ... for something to *do.*

MAN. I'll be in the pool ... if you need me.

ANN. You've got it backwards. People your age *leave* Manhattan.

49

They come *here*.

MARJORIE. I'm a late starter.

MAN. *(Breaks into a sudden Charleston.)* "Lets start jivin'
    Lets start divin'
    Everyone in the pool." That one never sold, either. *(He exits.)*

ANN. Well, it's your life.

MARJORIE. And it's only taken us six decades to figure that out.

ANN. So, you're just going to sell "The Place".

MARJORIE. No, no. Tony and Joy can live here if they so desire. And you can let your progeny shinny up every tree twelve times over.

ANN. *(Beaming.)* Mother!

MARJORIE. And you can pay me a very substantial rent for the privilege.

ANN. But ... but Tony could never afford —

MARJORIE. Well, you and Tony will just have to figure that out for yourselves, won't you? I'll expect a little check ... no, I'll expect a *big* check in the mail each month. And if you can't afford it, I'm sure I can find someone else who can.

ANN. You're treating us like ... like ...

MARJORIE. Adults?

ANN. Strangers!

MARJORIE. Well, they say one should never do business with family. Anyway, it's not as if I'll be far away.

ANN. Manhattan! You'll hate it. You won't last a month.

MARJORIE. Oh yes, it will be difficult. I hope. You see, Ann, it has suddenly occurred to me that New Zealand was an escape. A running away. And that's not what I want. No more easy choices ... *(She looks off towards the pool.)* Jack isn't here anymore...

ANN. He hasn't been here for quite a while, mother.

MARJORIE. No, I mean ... Never mind. Manhattan, *yes.* And difficult? Very. How I look forward to that! And *I* shall be difficult, too. I intend to hurl myself into the city. When people ask me how I am, I'm going to *tell* them! Oh Ann, I cannot wait to be *rude.* And I shall join things. Real things. Not bridge clubs or garden clubs, but *groups.* People out to change things. And I'll be able to subscribe to the Met! *And* to the Mets!! You and Tony can settle in here and cultivate children to your hearts' content, but count me out.

50

That chapter of my book is closed … *(Looking at Brian.)* Now as for this fellow, I suggest you take him home and have a long talk.

BRIAN. *(Waking.)* Do you know how long a long talk with Ann can be?

MARJORIE. Some people call that a marriage.

ANN. *(To Brian.)* You've been listening to every word.

BRIAN. Maybe. Or maybe it was all a dream. *(He dozes off again.)*

ANN. But what about the upkeep? The pool, the lawns. I'm busy and Tony is hopeless.

MARJORIE. Entirely your domain, my pet. After all, it was your idea.

ANN. It was my idea that you would be here *with* us.

MARJORIE. That's right. *(Smiling — sweetly.)* And I almost fell for it.

ANN. *(Angry.)* I'm going now.

MARJORIE. Try not to be bitter, Ann. Something went awry, that's all. In your great scheme of things. I love you very much. I just assume you know that. Does it have, continually, to be said?

ANN. "Something went awry!?" A little more than that, Mother. Someone said … Someone who died said — "You know when God laughs? When you start making plans." He's laughing at me, I suppose. Do you suppose He's laughing at you? *(Pause.)*

MARJORIE. I am amazed you think God is a man.

ANN. *(Angry.)* Now I *am* going.

MARJORIE. Well take your John Bull with you, please.

ANN. No. He's more than I can deal with tonight. He's got some overnight things in the blue bedroom.

MARJORIE. Ann …

ANN. Goodnight, Mother. I think you're being very difficult.

MARJORIE. Ohh … I hope so.

ANN. I can't imagine what Father would say.

MARJORIE. Well, I can, and it's not terribly interesting.

ANN. About Tony and the other business with Will Perry —

MARJORIE. Tony's business. Not mine.

ANN. God save us all from liberated matrons!

MARJORIE. Why, Ann. How very old-fashioned you've become. *(Ann stalks out.)* Brian? *(No reply. He is really zonked out now.)* Blue bedroom be damned, you can sleep out here. *(The sound of Ann's*

51

car leaving. The sky is darkening to dusk.) And you're gone too, aren't you Jack? *(Phone on table rings. Marjorie answers.)* Hello? Mr. Palestrina, how nice to hear from you. Tony told you to phone? Yes, I'm sure he did. Mr. Palestrina, could you drop by here tomorrow … Good. I want you to *drain* the pool … That's right; bone dry … But I have no intention of using it again … Well, look at it this way: Mr. Palestrina, it'll give you more time for your music. *(Marjorie hangs up the phone. Pause.)* No one to talk to. *(Joy strolls on from R.)* Joy! Darling how did you get here?

JOY. Walked.

MARJORIE. From Healey's?

JOY. Isn't far. *(She sees Brian.)* Oh … he's here.

MARJORIE. Not really. The Old World is sound asleep.

JOY. Brian and Ann left me there in the bar. I waited. Then I thought: What am I waiting for? Really? I mean, what am I, really waiting for? I knew Tony would come bounding back in. I suddenly didn't want to see him do that. Bound back in. So I left and started walking. Of course, I walked here. Where else to go?

MARJORIE. Oh, *everywhere.*

JOY. What?

MARJORIE. There is everywhere for you to go, Joy. I've learned that from you: Dive right in.

JOY. Marjorie … I have two children to raise.

MARJORIE. And you will. Annie says we can "have it all." She's having second thoughts right now, but at least we're all *having* thoughts, which we never used to.

JOY. I see. *(Pause.)* You've told me nothing. What's going on?

MARJORIE. Oh, I'll tell you everything. I have so much planning to do. Planning and packing …

JOY. Marjorie … *(Marjorie goes to Joy and takes her hand.)*

MARJORIE. I want you to stay. Just for a little while. I'm going to need help. I'll be moving soon.

JOY. And "The Place"?

MARJORIE. That's for Tony and Ann to deal with. Or, not deal with. Like grownups.

JOY. I see.

MARJORIE. Sit down, Joy. Sit and stay with me awhile. You're the one person I want to have stay with me. *(Joy is not sure what to*

52

do. She looks nervously at Brian.)

MARJORIE. Don't worry about him. We must all stop worrying about men who aren't really there. Now, do sit.

JOY. Well, I ... Thank you. For a while, yes. *(She sits.)* I must look a fright. *(She takes a comb out of her purse.)*

MARJORIE. Let me do that.

JOY. What?

MARJORIE. Let me comb out your long, beautiful hair. I have always wanted to do that, but I've been too shy to ask. May I? May I comb out your beautiful hair?

JOY. Well, yes. If you like. *(They sit in the darkening evening, the older woman combing out the younger woman's raven black hair. The phone rings.)* That will be Tony. *(Joy moves to answer it.)*

MARJORIE. Let it ring. *(She continues combing Joy's hair.)* Let freedom ring ... *(Lights Fade Slowly to Black ...)*

End of Play

PROPERTY LIST

Book (MARJORIE)
Enormous bag (ANN)
Ice bucket (ANN)
Large bottle mineral water (ANN)

SOUND EFFECTS

Car entering driveway
Car leaving driveway
Large splash
Splashes
Siren
Rolling thunder
Phone ringing

NEW PLAYS

★ **HONOUR by Joanna Murray-Smith.** In a series of intense confrontations, a wife, husband, lover and daughter negotiate the forces of passion, history, responsibility and honour. "HONOUR makes for surprisingly interesting viewing. Tight, crackling dialogue (usually played out in punchy verbal duels) captures characters unable to deal with emotions ... Murray-Smith effectively places her characters in situations that strip away pretense." –*Variety* "... the play's virtues are strong: a distinctive theatrical voice, passionate concerns ... HONOUR might just capture a few honors of its own." –*Time Out Magazine* [1M, 3W] ISBN: 0-8222-1683-3

★ **MR. PETERS' CONNECTIONS by Arthur Miller.** Mr. Miller describes the protagonist as existing in a dream-like state when the mind is "freed to roam from real memories to conjectures, from trivialities to tragic insights, from terror of death to glorying in one's being alive." With this memory play, the Tony Award and Pulitzer Prize-winner reaffirms his stature as the world's foremost dramatist. "... a cross between Joycean stream-of-consciousness and Strindberg's dream plays, sweetened with a dose of William Saroyan's philosophical whimsy ... CONNECTIONS is most intriguing ..." –*The NY Times* [5M, 3W] ISBN: 0-8222-1687-6

★ **THE WAITING ROOM by Lisa Loomer.** Three women from different centuries meet in a doctor's waiting room in this dark comedy about the timeless quest for beauty – and its cost. "... THE WAITING ROOM ... is a bold, risky melange of conflicting elements that is ... terrifically moving ... There's no resisting the fierce emotional pull of the play." –*The NY Times* "... one of the high points of this year's Off-Broadway season ... THE WAITING ROOM is well worth a visit." –*Back Stage* [7M, 4W, flexible casting] ISBN: 0-8222-1594-2

★ **THE OLD SETTLER by John Henry Redwood.** A sweet-natured comedy about two church-going sisters in 1943 Harlem and the handsome young man who rents a room in their apartment. "For all of its decent sentiments, THE OLD SETTLER avoids sentimentality. It has the authenticity and lack of pretense of an Early American sampler." –*The NY Times* "We've had some fine plays Off-Broadway this season, and this is one of the best." –*The NY Post* [1M, 3W] ISBN: 0-8-222-1642-6

★ **LAST TRAIN TO NIBROC by Arlene Hutton.** In 1940 two young strangers share a seat on a train bound east only to find their paths will cross again. "All aboard. LAST TRAIN TO NIBROC is a sweetly told little chamber romance." –*Show Business* "... [a] gently charming little play, reminiscent of Thornton Wilder in its look at rustic Americans who are to be treasured for their simplicity and directness ..." –*Associated Press* "The old formula of boy wins girls, boy loses girl, boy wins girl still works ... [a] well-made play that perfectly captures a slice of small-town-life-gone-by." –*Back Stage* [1M, 1W] ISBN: 0-8222-1753-8

★ **OVER THE RIVER AND THROUGH THE WOODS by Joe DiPietro.** Nick sees both sets of his grandparents every Sunday for dinner. This is routine until he has to tell them that he's been offered a dream job in Seattle. The news doesn't sit so well. "A hilarious family comedy that is even funnier than his long running musical revue *I Love You, You're Perfect, Now Change*." –*Back Stage* "Loaded with laughs every step of the way." –*Star-Ledger* [3M, 3W] ISBN: 0-8222-1712-0

★ **SIDE MAN by Warren Leight.** 1999 Tony Award winner. This is the story of a broken family and the decline of jazz as popular entertainment. "... a tender, deeply personal memory play about the turmoil in the family of a jazz musician as his career crumbles at the dawn of the age of rock-and-roll ..." –*The NY Times* "[SIDE MAN] is an elegy for two things – a lost world and a lost love. When the two notes sound together in harmony, it is moving and graceful ..." –*The NY Daily News* "An atmospheric memory play ... with crisp dialogue and clearly drawn characters ... reflects the passing of an era with persuasive insight ... The joy and despair of the musicians is skillfully illustrated." –*Variety* [5M, 3W] ISBN: 0-8222-1721-X

DRAMATISTS PLAY SERVICE, INC.
440 Park Avenue South, New York, NY 10016 212-683-8960 Fax 212-213-1539
postmaster@dramatists.com   www.dramatists.com

NEW PLAYS

★ **CLOSER by Patrick Marber.** Winner of the 1998 Olivier Award for Best Play and the 1999 New York Drama Critics Circle Award for Best Foreign Play. Four lives intertwine over the course of four and a half years in this densely plotted, stinging look at modern love and betrayal. "CLOSER is a sad, savvy, often funny play that casts a steely, unblinking gaze at the world of relationships and lets you come to your own conclusions ... CLOSER does not merely hold your attention; it burrows into you." –*New York Magazine* "A powerful, darkly funny play about the cosmic collision between the sun of love and the comet of desire." –*Newsweek Magazine* [2M, 2W] ISBN: 0-8222-1722-8

★ **THE MOST FABULOUS STORY EVER TOLD by Paul Rudnick.** A stage manager, headset and prompt book at hand, brings the house lights to half, then dark, and cues the creation of the world. Throughout the play, she's in control of everything. In other words, she's either God, or she thinks she is. "Line by line, Mr. Rudnick may be the funniest writer for the stage in the United States today ... One-liners, epigrams, withering put-downs and flashing repartee: These are the candles that Mr. Rudnick lights instead of cursing the darkness ... a testament to the virtues of laughing ... and in laughter, there is something like the memory of Eden." –*The NY Times* "Funny it is ... consistently, rapaciously, deliriously ... easily the funniest play in town." –*Variety* [4M, 5W] ISBN: 0-8222-1720-1

★ **A DOLL'S HOUSE by Henrik Ibsen, adapted by Frank McGuinness.** Winner of the 1997 Tony Award for Best Revival. "New, raw, gut-twisting and gripping. Easily the hottest drama this season." –*USA Today* "Bold, brilliant and alive." –*The Wall Street Journal* "A thunderclap of an evening that takes your breath away." –*Time Magazine* [4M, 4W, 2 boys] ISBN: 0-8222-1636-1

★ **THE HERBAL BED by Peter Whelan.** The play is based on actual events which occurred in Stratford-upon-Avon in the summer of 1613, when William Shakespeare's elder daughter was publicly accused of having a sexual liaison with a married neighbor and family friend. "In his probing new play, THE HERBAL BED ... Peter Whelan muses about a sidelong event in the life of Shakespeare's family and creates a finely textured tapestry of love and lies in the early 17th-century Stratford." –*The NY Times* "It is a first rate drama with interesting moral issues of truth and expediency." –*The NY Post* [5M, 3W] ISBN: 0-8222-1675-2

★ **SNAKEBIT by David Marshall Grant.** A study of modern friendship when put to the test. "... a rather smart and absorbing evening of water-cooler theater, the intimate sort of Off-Broadway experience that has you picking apart the recognizable characters long after the curtain calls." –*The NY Times* "Off-Broadway keeps on presenting us with compelling reasons for going to the theater. The latest is SNAKEBIT, David Marshall Grant's smart new comic drama about being thirtysomething and losing one's way in life." –*The NY Daily News* [3M, 1W] ISBN: 0-8222-1724-4

★ **A QUESTION OF MERCY by David Rabe.** The Obie Award-winning playwright probes the sensitive and controversial issue of doctor-assisted suicide in the age of AIDS in this poignant drama. "There are many devastating ironies in Mr. Rabe's beautifully considered, piercingly clear-eyed work ..." –*The NY Times* "With unsettling candor and disturbing insight, the play arouses pity and understanding of a troubling subject ... Rabe's provocative tale is an affirmation of dignity that rings clear and true." –*Variety* [6M, 1W] ISBN: 0-8222-1643-4

★ **DIMLY PERCEIVED THREATS TO THE SYSTEM by Jon Klein.** Reality and fantasy overlap with hilarious results as this unforgettable family attempts to survive the nineties. "Here's a play whose point about fractured families goes to the heart, mind – and ears." –*The Washington Post* "... an end-of-the millennium comedy about a family on the verge of a nervous breakdown ... Trenchant and hilarious ..." –*The Baltimore Sun* [2M, 4W] ISBN: 0-8222-1677-9

DRAMATISTS PLAY SERVICE, INC.
440 Park Avenue South, New York, NY 10016 212-683-8960 Fax 212-213-1539
postmaster@dramatists.com www.dramatists.com

NEW PLAYS

★ **AS BEES IN HONEY DROWN by Douglas Carter Beane.** Winner of the John Gassner Playwriting Award. A hot young novelist finds the subject of his new screenplay in a New York socialite who leads him into the world of *Auntie Mame* and *Breakfast at Tiffany's*, before she takes him for a ride. "A delicious soufflé of a satire ... [an] extremely entertaining fable for an age that always chooses image over substance." –*The NY Times* "... A witty assessment of one of the most active and relentless industries in a consumer society ... the creation of 'hot' young things, which the media have learned to mass produce with efficiency and zeal." –*The NY Daily News* [3M, 3W, flexible casting] ISBN: 0-8222-1651-5

★ **STUPID KIDS by John C. Russell.** In rapid, highly stylized scenes, the story follows four high-school students as they make their way from first through eighth period and beyond, struggling with the fears, frustrations, and longings peculiar to youth. "In STUPID KIDS ... playwright John C. Russell gets the opera of adolescence to a T ... The stylized teenspeak of STUPID KIDS ... suggests that Mr. Russell may have hidden a tape recorder under a desk in study hall somewhere and then scoured the tapes for good quotations ... it is the kids' insular, ceaselessly churning world, a pre-adult world of Doritos and libidos, that the playwright seeks to lay bare." –*The NY Times* "STUPID KIDS [is] a sharp-edged ... whoosh of teen angst and conformity anguish. It is also very funny." –*NY Newsday* [2M, 2W] ISBN: 0-8222-1698-1

★ **COLLECTED STORIES by Donald Margulies.** From Obie Award-winner Donald Margulies comes a provocative analysis of a student-teacher relationship that turns sour when the protégé becomes a rival. "With his fine ear for detail, Margulies creates an authentic, insular world, and he gives equal weight to the opposing viewpoints of two formidable characters." –*The LA Times* "This is probably Margulies' best play to date ..." –*The NY Post* "... always fluid and lively, the play is thick with ideas, like a stock-pot of good stew." –*The Village Voice* [2W] ISBN: 0-8222-1640-X

★ **FREEDOMLAND by Amy Freed.** An overdue showdown between a son and his father sets off fireworks that illuminate the neurosis, rage and anxiety of one family – and of America at the turn of the millennium. "FREEDOMLAND's more obvious links are to *Buried Child* and *Bosoms and Neglect*. Freed, like Guare, is an inspired wordsmith with a gift for surreal touches in situations grounded in familiar and real territory." –*Curtain Up* [3M, 4W] ISBN: 0-8222-1719-8

★ **STOP KISS by Diana Son.** A poignant and funny play about the ways, both sudden and slow, that lives can change irrevocably. "There's so much that is vital and exciting about STOP KISS ... you want to embrace this young author and cheer her onto other works ... the writing on display here is funny and credible ... you also will be charmed by its heartfelt characters and up-to-the-minute humor." –*The NY Daily News* "... irresistibly exciting ... a sweet, sad, and enchantingly sincere play." –*The NY Times* [3M, 3W] ISBN: 0-8222-1731-7

★ **THREE DAYS OF RAIN by Richard Greenberg.** The sins of fathers and mothers make for a bittersweet elegy in this poignant and revealing drama. "... a work so perfectly judged it heralds the arrival of a major playwright ... Greenberg is extraordinary." –*The NY Daily News* "Greenberg's play is filled with graceful passages that are by turns melancholy, harrowing, and often, quite funny." –*Variety* [2M, 1W] ISBN: 0-8222-1676-0

★ **THE WEIR by Conor McPherson.** In a bar in rural Ireland, the local men swap spooky stories in an attempt to impress a young woman from Dublin who recently moved into a nearby "haunted" house. However, the tables are soon turned when she spins a yarn of her own. "You shed all sense of time at this beautiful and devious new play." –*The NY Times* "Sheer theatrical magic. I have rarely been so convinced that I have just seen a modern classic. Tremendous." –*The London Daily Telegraph* [4M, 1W] ISBN: 0-8222-1706-6

DRAMATISTS PLAY SERVICE, INC.
440 Park Avenue South, New York, NY 10016 212-683-8960 Fax 212-213-1539
postmaster@dramatists.com   www.dramatists.com